THE ACCIDENT LOG BOOK

HEALTH & SAFETY INCIDENT RECORD BOOK

COMPANY & LOG BOOK DETAILS		
Log Start Date:		**Log Book No.**
Name:		
Address:		
Email:		
Telephone No.		
Emergency Contact:		

Published by
Accident Log & Incident Report Books Publishing

ACCIDENT / INCIDENT REPORT FORM

Incident Date:		Reported by:			Report Date:	
Incident Time:		Location:				

Person Involved /Injured:	Employee	Contractor	Visitor	General Public	Member	Other
Full Name:						
Address:						
Tel:			Email:			

DESCRIPTION OF ACCIDENT / INCIDENT

ACTION TAKEN / ACTIONS WHICH MAY PREVENT FUTURE REOCCURRENCE

WITNESS/ES

Full Name:		Contact:	
Full Name:		Contact:	
Full Name:		Contact:	
Form Completed by:		Signed:	
Approved by:		Signed:	

ACCIDENT / INCIDENT REPORT FORM

Incident Date:		Reported by:		Report Date:	
Incident Time:		Location:			

Person Involved /Injured:	Employee	Contractor	Visitor	General Public	Member	Other
Full Name:						
Address:						
Tel:		Email:				

DESCRIPTION OF ACCIDENT / INCIDENT

ACTION TAKEN / ACTIONS WHICH MAY PREVENT FUTURE REOCCURRENCE

WITNESS/ES

Full Name:		Contact:	
Full Name:		Contact:	
Full Name:		Contact:	
Form Completed by:		Signed:	
Approved by:		Signed:	

ACCIDENT / INCIDENT REPORT FORM

Incident Date:		Reported by:			Report Date:	
Incident Time:		Location:				

Person Involved /Injured:	Employee	Contractor	Visitor	General Public	Member	Other
Full Name:						
Address:						
Tel:			Email:			

DESCRIPTION OF ACCIDENT / INCIDENT

ACTION TAKEN / ACTIONS WHICH MAY PREVENT FUTURE REOCCURRENCE

WITNESS/ES

Full Name:		Contact:	
Full Name:		Contact:	
Full Name:		Contact:	
Form Completed by:		Signed:	
Approved by:		Signed:	

ACCIDENT / INCIDENT REPORT FORM

Incident Date:		Reported by:		Report Date:	
Incident Time:		Location:			

Person Involved /Injured:	Employee	Contractor	Visitor	General Public	Member	Other
Full Name:						
Address:						
Tel:		Email:				

DESCRIPTION OF ACCIDENT / INCIDENT

ACTION TAKEN / ACTIONS WHICH MAY PREVENT FUTURE REOCCURRENCE

WITNESS/ES

Full Name:		Contact:	
Full Name:		Contact:	
Full Name:		Contact:	
Form Completed by:		Signed:	
Approved by:		Signed:	

ACCIDENT / INCIDENT REPORT FORM

Incident Date:		Reported by:		Report Date:	
Incident Time:		Location:			

Person Involved /Injured:	Employee	Contractor	Visitor	General Public	Member	Other
Full Name:						
Address:						
Tel:			Email:			

DESCRIPTION OF ACCIDENT / INCIDENT

ACTION TAKEN / ACTIONS WHICH MAY PREVENT FUTURE REOCCURRENCE

WITNESS/ES

Full Name:		Contact:	
Full Name:		Contact:	
Full Name:		Contact:	
Form Completed by:		Signed:	
Approved by:		Signed:	

ACCIDENT / INCIDENT REPORT FORM

Incident Date:		Reported by:		Report Date:	
Incident Time:		Location:			

Person Involved /Injured:	Employee	Contractor	Visitor	General Public	Member	Other
Full Name:						
Address:						
Tel:			Email:			

DESCRIPTION OF ACCIDENT / INCIDENT

ACTION TAKEN / ACTIONS WHICH MAY PREVENT FUTURE REOCCURRENCE

WITNESS/ES

Full Name:		Contact:	
Full Name:		Contact:	
Full Name:		Contact:	
Form Completed by:		Signed:	
Approved by:		Signed:	

ACCIDENT / INCIDENT REPORT FORM

Incident Date:		Reported by:			Report Date:	
Incident Time:		Location:				

Person Involved /Injured:	Employee	Contractor	Visitor	General Public	Member	Other
Full Name:						
Address:						
Tel:			Email:			

DESCRIPTION OF ACCIDENT / INCIDENT

ACTION TAKEN / ACTIONS WHICH MAY PREVENT FUTURE REOCCURRENCE

WITNESS/ES

Full Name:		Contact:	
Full Name:		Contact:	
Full Name:		Contact:	
Form Completed by:		Signed:	
Approved by:		Signed:	

ACCIDENT / INCIDENT REPORT FORM

Incident Date:		Reported by:		Report Date:	
Incident Time:		Location:			

Person Involved /Injured:	Employee	Contractor	Visitor	General Public	Member	Other
Full Name:						
Address:						
Tel:		Email:				

DESCRIPTION OF ACCIDENT / INCIDENT

ACTION TAKEN / ACTIONS WHICH MAY PREVENT FUTURE REOCCURRENCE

WITNESS/ES

Full Name:		Contact:	
Full Name:		Contact:	
Full Name:		Contact:	
Form Completed by:		Signed:	
Approved by:		Signed:	

ACCIDENT / INCIDENT REPORT FORM

Incident Date:		Reported by:			Report Date:	
Incident Time:		Location:				

Person Involved /Injured:	Employee	Contractor	Visitor	General Public	Member	Other
Full Name:						
Address:						
Tel:			Email:			

DESCRIPTION OF ACCIDENT / INCIDENT

ACTION TAKEN / ACTIONS WHICH MAY PREVENT FUTURE REOCCURRENCE

WITNESS/ES

Full Name:		Contact:	
Full Name:		Contact:	
Full Name:		Contact:	
Form Completed by:		Signed:	
Approved by:		Signed:	

ACCIDENT / INCIDENT REPORT FORM

Incident Date:		Reported by:			Report Date:	

Incident Time:		Location:				

Person Involved /Injured:	Employee	Contractor	Visitor	General Public	Member	Other
Full Name:						
Address:						
Tel:			Email:			

DESCRIPTION OF ACCIDENT / INCIDENT

ACTION TAKEN / ACTIONS WHICH MAY PREVENT FUTURE REOCCURRENCE

WITNESS/ES

Full Name:		Contact:	
Full Name:		Contact:	
Full Name:		Contact:	
Form Completed by:		Signed:	
Approved by:		Signed:	

ACCIDENT / INCIDENT REPORT FORM

Incident Date:		Reported by:			Report Date:	
Incident Time:		Location:				

Person Involved /Injured:	Employee	Contractor	Visitor	General Public	Member	Other
Full Name:						
Address:						
Tel:		Email:				

DESCRIPTION OF ACCIDENT / INCIDENT

ACTION TAKEN / ACTIONS WHICH MAY PREVENT FUTURE REOCCURRENCE

WITNESS/ES

Full Name:		Contact:	
Full Name:		Contact:	
Full Name:		Contact:	
Form Completed by:		Signed:	
Approved by:		Signed:	

ACCIDENT / INCIDENT REPORT FORM

| Incident Date: | | Reported by: | | Report Date: | |

| Incident Time: | | Location: | |

Person Involved /Injured:	Employee	Contractor	Visitor	General Public	Member	Other
Full Name:						
Address:						
Tel:		Email:				

DESCRIPTION OF ACCIDENT / INCIDENT

ACTION TAKEN / ACTIONS WHICH MAY PREVENT FUTURE REOCCURRENCE

WITNESS/ES

Full Name:		Contact:	
Full Name:		Contact:	
Full Name:		Contact:	
Form Completed by:		Signed:	
Approved by:		Signed:	

ACCIDENT / INCIDENT REPORT FORM

Incident Date:		Reported by:		Report Date:	
Incident Time:		Location:			

Person Involved /Injured:	Employee	Contractor	Visitor	General Public	Member	Other
Full Name:						
Address:						
Tel:		Email:				

DESCRIPTION OF ACCIDENT / INCIDENT

ACTION TAKEN / ACTIONS WHICH MAY PREVENT FUTURE REOCCURRENCE

WITNESS/ES

Full Name:		Contact:	
Full Name:		Contact:	
Full Name:		Contact:	
Form Completed by:		Signed:	
Approved by:		Signed:	

ACCIDENT / INCIDENT REPORT FORM

Incident Date:		Reported by:			Report Date:	
Incident Time:		Location:				

Person Involved /Injured:	Employee	Contractor	Visitor	General Public	Member	Other
Full Name:						
Address:						
Tel:			Email:			

DESCRIPTION OF ACCIDENT / INCIDENT

ACTION TAKEN / ACTIONS WHICH MAY PREVENT FUTURE REOCCURRENCE

WITNESS/ES

Full Name:		Contact:	
Full Name:		Contact:	
Full Name:		Contact:	
Form Completed by:		Signed:	
Approved by:		Signed:	

ACCIDENT / INCIDENT REPORT FORM

Incident Date:		Reported by:			Report Date:	
Incident Time:		Location:				

Person Involved /Injured:	Employee	Contractor	Visitor	General Public	Member	Other
Full Name:						
Address:						
Tel:			Email:			

DESCRIPTION OF ACCIDENT / INCIDENT

ACTION TAKEN / ACTIONS WHICH MAY PREVENT FUTURE REOCCURRENCE

WITNESS/ES

Full Name:		Contact:	
Full Name:		Contact:	
Full Name:		Contact:	
Form Completed by:		Signed:	
Approved by:		Signed:	

ACCIDENT / INCIDENT REPORT FORM

Incident Date:		Reported by:			Report Date:	
Incident Time:		Location:				

Person Involved /Injured:	Employee	Contractor	Visitor	General Public	Member	Other
Full Name:						
Address:						
Tel:			Email:			

DESCRIPTION OF ACCIDENT / INCIDENT

ACTION TAKEN / ACTIONS WHICH MAY PREVENT FUTURE REOCCURRENCE

WITNESS/ES

Full Name:		Contact:	
Full Name:		Contact:	
Full Name:		Contact:	
Form Completed by:		Signed:	
Approved by:		Signed:	

ACCIDENT / INCIDENT REPORT FORM

| Incident Date: | | Reported by: | | Report Date: | |

| Incident Time: | | Location: | |

Person Involved /Injured:	Employee	Contractor	Visitor	General Public	Member	Other
Full Name:						
Address:						
Tel:		Email:				

DESCRIPTION OF ACCIDENT / INCIDENT

ACTION TAKEN / ACTIONS WHICH MAY PREVENT FUTURE REOCCURRENCE

WITNESS/ES

Full Name:		Contact:	
Full Name:		Contact:	
Full Name:		Contact:	
Form Completed by:		Signed:	
Approved by:		Signed:	

ACCIDENT / INCIDENT REPORT FORM

Incident Date:		Reported by:			Report Date:	
Incident Time:		Location:				

Person Involved /Injured:	Employee	Contractor	Visitor	General Public	Member	Other
Full Name:						
Address:						
Tel:			Email:			

DESCRIPTION OF ACCIDENT / INCIDENT

ACTION TAKEN / ACTIONS WHICH MAY PREVENT FUTURE REOCCURRENCE

WITNESS/ES

Full Name:		Contact:	
Full Name:		Contact:	
Full Name:		Contact:	
Form Completed by:		Signed:	
Approved by:		Signed:	

ACCIDENT / INCIDENT REPORT FORM

Incident Date:		Reported by:		Report Date:	
Incident Time:		Location:			

Person Involved /Injured:	Employee	Contractor	Visitor	General Public	Member	Other
Full Name:						
Address:						
Tel:		Email:				

DESCRIPTION OF ACCIDENT / INCIDENT

ACTION TAKEN / ACTIONS WHICH MAY PREVENT FUTURE REOCCURRENCE

WITNESS/ES

Full Name:		Contact:	
Full Name:		Contact:	
Full Name:		Contact:	
Form Completed by:		Signed:	
Approved by:		Signed:	

ACCIDENT / INCIDENT REPORT FORM

Incident Date:		Reported by:		Report Date:	
Incident Time:		Location:			

Person Involved /Injured:	Employee	Contractor	Visitor	General Public	Member	Other
Full Name:						
Address:						
Tel:		Email:				

DESCRIPTION OF ACCIDENT / INCIDENT

ACTION TAKEN / ACTIONS WHICH MAY PREVENT FUTURE REOCCURRENCE

WITNESS/ES

Full Name:		Contact:	
Full Name:		Contact:	
Full Name:		Contact:	
Form Completed by:		Signed:	
Approved by:		Signed:	

ACCIDENT / INCIDENT REPORT FORM

Incident Date:		Reported by:		Report Date:	
Incident Time:		Location:			

Person Involved /Injured:	Employee	Contractor	Visitor	General Public	Member	Other
Full Name:						
Address:						
Tel:			Email:			

DESCRIPTION OF ACCIDENT / INCIDENT

ACTION TAKEN / ACTIONS WHICH MAY PREVENT FUTURE REOCCURRENCE

WITNESS/ES

Full Name:		Contact:	
Full Name:		Contact:	
Full Name:		Contact:	
Form Completed by:		Signed:	
Approved by:		Signed:	

ACCIDENT / INCIDENT REPORT FORM

Incident Date:		Reported by:		Report Date:	
Incident Time:		Location:			

Person Involved /Injured:	Employee	Contractor	Visitor	General Public	Member	Other
Full Name:						
Address:						
Tel:		Email:				

DESCRIPTION OF ACCIDENT / INCIDENT

ACTION TAKEN / ACTIONS WHICH MAY PREVENT FUTURE REOCCURRENCE

WITNESS/ES

Full Name:		Contact:	
Full Name:		Contact:	
Full Name:		Contact:	
Form Completed by:		Signed:	
Approved by:		Signed:	

ACCIDENT / INCIDENT REPORT FORM

Incident Date:		Reported by:			Report Date:	

Incident Time:		Location:	

Person Involved /Injured:	Employee	Contractor	Visitor	General Public	Member	Other
Full Name:						
Address:						

Tel:		Email:	

DESCRIPTION OF ACCIDENT / INCIDENT

ACTION TAKEN / ACTIONS WHICH MAY PREVENT FUTURE REOCCURRENCE

WITNESS/ES

Full Name:		Contact:	
Full Name:		Contact:	
Full Name:		Contact:	
Form Completed by:		Signed:	
Approved by:		Signed:	

ACCIDENT / INCIDENT REPORT FORM

Incident Date:		Reported by:		Report Date:	
Incident Time:		Location:			

Person Involved /Injured:	Employee	Contractor	Visitor	General Public	Member	Other
Full Name:						
Address:						
Tel:			Email:			

DESCRIPTION OF ACCIDENT / INCIDENT

ACTION TAKEN / ACTIONS WHICH MAY PREVENT FUTURE REOCCURRENCE

WITNESS/ES

Full Name:		Contact:	
Full Name:		Contact:	
Full Name:		Contact:	
Form Completed by:		Signed:	
Approved by:		Signed:	

ACCIDENT / INCIDENT REPORT FORM

Incident Date:		Reported by:				Report Date:	
Incident Time:		Location:					

Person Involved /Injured:	Employee	Contractor	Visitor	General Public	Member	Other
Full Name:						
Address:						
Tel:			Email:			

DESCRIPTION OF ACCIDENT / INCIDENT

ACTION TAKEN / ACTIONS WHICH MAY PREVENT FUTURE REOCCURRENCE

WITNESS/ES

Full Name:		Contact:	
Full Name:		Contact:	
Full Name:		Contact:	
Form Completed by:		Signed:	
Approved by:		Signed:	

ACCIDENT / INCIDENT REPORT FORM

Incident Date:		Reported by:		Report Date:	

Incident Time:		Location:			

Person Involved /Injured:	Employee	Contractor	Visitor	General Public	Member	Other

Full Name:	
Address:	

Tel:		Email:	

DESCRIPTION OF ACCIDENT / INCIDENT

ACTION TAKEN / ACTIONS WHICH MAY PREVENT FUTURE REOCCURRENCE

WITNESS/ES

Full Name:		Contact:	
Full Name:		Contact:	
Full Name:		Contact:	

Form Completed by:		Signed:	
Approved by:		Signed:	

ACCIDENT / INCIDENT REPORT FORM

Incident Date:		Reported by:			Report Date:	
Incident Time:		Location:				

Person Involved /Injured:	Employee	Contractor	Visitor	General Public	Member	Other
Full Name:						
Address:						
Tel:			Email:			

DESCRIPTION OF ACCIDENT / INCIDENT

ACTION TAKEN / ACTIONS WHICH MAY PREVENT FUTURE REOCCURRENCE

WITNESS/ES

Full Name:		Contact:	
Full Name:		Contact:	
Full Name:		Contact:	
Form Completed by:		Signed:	
Approved by:		Signed:	

ACCIDENT / INCIDENT REPORT FORM

Incident Date:		Reported by:			Report Date:	
Incident Time:		Location:				

Person Involved /Injured:	Employee	Contractor	Visitor	General Public	Member	Other
Full Name:						
Address:						
Tel:			Email:			

DESCRIPTION OF ACCIDENT / INCIDENT

ACTION TAKEN / ACTIONS WHICH MAY PREVENT FUTURE REOCCURRENCE

WITNESS/ES

Full Name:		Contact:	
Full Name:		Contact:	
Full Name:		Contact:	
Form Completed by:		Signed:	
Approved by:		Signed:	

ACCIDENT / INCIDENT REPORT FORM

| Incident Date: | | Reported by: | | | Report Date: | |

| Incident Time: | | Location: | | | | |

Person Involved /Injured:	Employee	Contractor	Visitor	General Public	Member	Other
Full Name:						
Address:						
Tel:			Email:			

DESCRIPTION OF ACCIDENT / INCIDENT

ACTION TAKEN / ACTIONS WHICH MAY PREVENT FUTURE REOCCURRENCE

WITNESS/ES

Full Name:		Contact:	
Full Name:		Contact:	
Full Name:		Contact:	
Form Completed by:		Signed:	
Approved by:		Signed:	

ACCIDENT / INCIDENT REPORT FORM

| Incident Date: | | Reported by: | | Report Date: | |
| Incident Time: | | Location: | | | |

Person Involved /Injured:	Employee	Contractor	Visitor	General Public	Member	Other
Full Name:						
Address:						
Tel:		Email:				

DESCRIPTION OF ACCIDENT / INCIDENT

ACTION TAKEN / ACTIONS WHICH MAY PREVENT FUTURE REOCCURRENCE

WITNESS/ES

Full Name:		Contact:	
Full Name:		Contact:	
Full Name:		Contact:	
Form Completed by:		Signed:	
Approved by:		Signed:	

ACCIDENT / INCIDENT REPORT FORM

Incident Date:		Reported by:			Report Date:	
Incident Time:		Location:				

Person Involved /Injured:	Employee	Contractor	Visitor	General Public	Member	Other
Full Name:						
Address:						
Tel:			Email:			

DESCRIPTION OF ACCIDENT / INCIDENT

ACTION TAKEN / ACTIONS WHICH MAY PREVENT FUTURE REOCCURRENCE

WITNESS/ES

Full Name:		Contact:	
Full Name:		Contact:	
Full Name:		Contact:	
Form Completed by:		Signed:	
Approved by:		Signed:	

ACCIDENT / INCIDENT REPORT FORM

Incident Date:		Reported by:			Report Date:	
Incident Time:		Location:				

Person Involved /Injured:	Employee	Contractor	Visitor	General Public	Member	Other
Full Name:						
Address:						
Tel:		Email:				

DESCRIPTION OF ACCIDENT / INCIDENT

ACTION TAKEN / ACTIONS WHICH MAY PREVENT FUTURE REOCCURRENCE

WITNESS/ES

Full Name:		Contact:	
Full Name:		Contact:	
Full Name:		Contact:	
Form Completed by:		Signed:	
Approved by:		Signed:	

ACCIDENT / INCIDENT REPORT FORM

Incident Date:		Reported by:			Report Date:	

Incident Time:		Location:				

Person Involved /Injured:	Employee	Contractor	Visitor	General Public	Member	Other
Full Name:						
Address:						
Tel:			Email:			

DESCRIPTION OF ACCIDENT / INCIDENT

ACTION TAKEN / ACTIONS WHICH MAY PREVENT FUTURE REOCCURRENCE

WITNESS/ES

Full Name:		Contact:	
Full Name:		Contact:	
Full Name:		Contact:	
Form Completed by:		Signed:	
Approved by:		Signed:	

ACCIDENT / INCIDENT REPORT FORM

Incident Date:		Reported by:		Report Date:	
Incident Time:		Location:			

Person Involved /Injured:	Employee	Contractor	Visitor	General Public	Member	Other
Full Name:						
Address:						
Tel:			Email:			

DESCRIPTION OF ACCIDENT / INCIDENT

ACTION TAKEN / ACTIONS WHICH MAY PREVENT FUTURE REOCCURRENCE

WITNESS/ES

Full Name:		Contact:	
Full Name:		Contact:	
Full Name:		Contact:	
Form Completed by:		Signed:	
Approved by:		Signed:	

ACCIDENT / INCIDENT REPORT FORM

Incident Date:		Reported by:			Report Date:	
Incident Time:		Location:				

Person Involved /Injured:	Employee	Contractor	Visitor	General Public	Member	Other
Full Name:						
Address:						
Tel:			Email:			

DESCRIPTION OF ACCIDENT / INCIDENT

ACTION TAKEN / ACTIONS WHICH MAY PREVENT FUTURE REOCCURRENCE

WITNESS/ES

Full Name:		Contact:	
Full Name:		Contact:	
Full Name:		Contact:	
Form Completed by:		Signed:	
Approved by:		Signed:	

ACCIDENT / INCIDENT REPORT FORM

Incident Date:		Reported by:			Report Date:	
Incident Time:		Location:				

Person Involved /Injured:	Employee	Contractor	Visitor	General Public	Member	Other
Full Name:						
Address:						
Tel:			Email:			

DESCRIPTION OF ACCIDENT / INCIDENT

ACTION TAKEN / ACTIONS WHICH MAY PREVENT FUTURE REOCCURRENCE

WITNESS/ES

Full Name:		Contact:	
Full Name:		Contact:	
Full Name:		Contact:	
Form Completed by:		Signed:	
Approved by:		Signed:	

ACCIDENT / INCIDENT REPORT FORM

Incident Date:		Reported by:			Report Date:	
Incident Time:		Location:				

Person Involved /Injured:	Employee	Contractor	Visitor	General Public	Member	Other
Full Name:						
Address:						
Tel:				Email:		

DESCRIPTION OF ACCIDENT / INCIDENT

ACTION TAKEN / ACTIONS WHICH MAY PREVENT FUTURE REOCCURRENCE

WITNESS/ES

Full Name:		Contact:	
Full Name:		Contact:	
Full Name:		Contact:	
Form Completed by:		Signed:	
Approved by:		Signed:	

ACCIDENT / INCIDENT REPORT FORM

| Incident Date: | | Reported by: | | | Report Date: | |
| Incident Time: | | Location: | | | | |

Person Involved /Injured:	Employee	Contractor	Visitor	General Public	Member	Other
Full Name:						
Address:						
Tel:			Email:			

DESCRIPTION OF ACCIDENT / INCIDENT

ACTION TAKEN / ACTIONS WHICH MAY PREVENT FUTURE REOCCURRENCE

WITNESS/ES

Full Name:		Contact:	
Full Name:		Contact:	
Full Name:		Contact:	
Form Completed by:		Signed:	
Approved by:		Signed:	

ACCIDENT / INCIDENT REPORT FORM

Incident Date:		Reported by:			Report Date:	
Incident Time:		Location:				

Person Involved /Injured:	Employee	Contractor	Visitor	General Public	Member	Other
Full Name:						
Address:						
Tel:			Email:			

DESCRIPTION OF ACCIDENT / INCIDENT

ACTION TAKEN / ACTIONS WHICH MAY PREVENT FUTURE REOCCURRENCE

WITNESS/ES

Full Name:		Contact:	
Full Name:		Contact:	
Full Name:		Contact:	
Form Completed by:		Signed:	
Approved by:		Signed:	

ACCIDENT / INCIDENT REPORT FORM

Incident Date:		Reported by:			Report Date:	
Incident Time:		Location:				

Person Involved /Injured:	Employee	Contractor	Visitor	General Public	Member	Other
Full Name:						
Address:						
Tel:			Email:			

DESCRIPTION OF ACCIDENT / INCIDENT

ACTION TAKEN / ACTIONS WHICH MAY PREVENT FUTURE REOCCURRENCE

WITNESS/ES

Full Name:		Contact:	
Full Name:		Contact:	
Full Name:		Contact:	
Form Completed by:		Signed:	
Approved by:		Signed:	

ACCIDENT / INCIDENT REPORT FORM

| Incident Date: | | Reported by: | | | Report Date: | |

| Incident Time: | | Location: | | | |

Person Involved /Injured:	Employee	Contractor	Visitor	General Public	Member	Other
Full Name:						
Address:						
Tel:			Email:			

DESCRIPTION OF ACCIDENT / INCIDENT

ACTION TAKEN / ACTIONS WHICH MAY PREVENT FUTURE REOCCURRENCE

WITNESS/ES

Full Name:		Contact:	
Full Name:		Contact:	
Full Name:		Contact:	
Form Completed by:		Signed:	
Approved by:		Signed:	

ACCIDENT / INCIDENT REPORT FORM

| Incident Date: | | Reported by: | | | Report Date: | |

| Incident Time: | | Location: | | | | |

Person Involved /Injured:	Employee	Contractor	Visitor	General Public	Member	Other
Full Name:						
Address:						
Tel:			Email:			

DESCRIPTION OF ACCIDENT / INCIDENT

ACTION TAKEN / ACTIONS WHICH MAY PREVENT FUTURE REOCCURRENCE

WITNESS/ES

Full Name:		Contact:	
Full Name:		Contact:	
Full Name:		Contact:	
Form Completed by:		Signed:	
Approved by:		Signed:	

ACCIDENT / INCIDENT REPORT FORM

Incident Date:		Reported by:			Report Date:	
Incident Time:		Location:				

Person Involved /Injured:	Employee	Contractor	Visitor	General Public	Member	Other
Full Name:						
Address:						
Tel:			Email:			

DESCRIPTION OF ACCIDENT / INCIDENT

ACTION TAKEN / ACTIONS WHICH MAY PREVENT FUTURE REOCCURRENCE

WITNESS/ES

Full Name:		Contact:	
Full Name:		Contact:	
Full Name:		Contact:	
Form Completed by:		Signed:	
Approved by:		Signed:	

ACCIDENT / INCIDENT REPORT FORM

Incident Date:		Reported by:			Report Date:	
Incident Time:		Location:				

Person Involved /Injured:	Employee	Contractor	Visitor	General Public	Member	Other
Full Name:						
Address:						
Tel:			Email:			

DESCRIPTION OF ACCIDENT / INCIDENT

ACTION TAKEN / ACTIONS WHICH MAY PREVENT FUTURE REOCCURRENCE

WITNESS/ES

Full Name:		Contact:	
Full Name:		Contact:	
Full Name:		Contact:	
Form Completed by:		Signed:	
Approved by:		Signed:	

ACCIDENT / INCIDENT REPORT FORM

Incident Date:		Reported by:			Report Date:	
Incident Time:		Location:				

Person Involved /Injured:	Employee	Contractor	Visitor	General Public	Member	Other
Full Name:						
Address:						
Tel:			Email:			

DESCRIPTION OF ACCIDENT / INCIDENT

ACTION TAKEN / ACTIONS WHICH MAY PREVENT FUTURE REOCCURRENCE

WITNESS/ES

Full Name:		Contact:	
Full Name:		Contact:	
Full Name:		Contact:	
Form Completed by:		Signed:	
Approved by:		Signed:	

ACCIDENT / INCIDENT REPORT FORM

Incident Date:		Reported by:			Report Date:	
Incident Time:		Location:				

Person Involved /Injured:	Employee	Contractor	Visitor	General Public	Member	Other
Full Name:						
Address:						
Tel:		Email:				

DESCRIPTION OF ACCIDENT / INCIDENT

ACTION TAKEN / ACTIONS WHICH MAY PREVENT FUTURE REOCCURRENCE

WITNESS/ES

Full Name:		Contact:	
Full Name:		Contact:	
Full Name:		Contact:	
Form Completed by:		Signed:	
Approved by:		Signed:	

ACCIDENT / INCIDENT REPORT FORM

| Incident Date: | | Reported by: | | | Report Date: | |

| Incident Time: | | Location: | | |

Person Involved /Injured:	Employee	Contractor	Visitor	General Public	Member	Other
Full Name:						
Address:						
Tel:			Email:			

DESCRIPTION OF ACCIDENT / INCIDENT

ACTION TAKEN / ACTIONS WHICH MAY PREVENT FUTURE REOCCURRENCE

WITNESS/ES

Full Name:		Contact:	
Full Name:		Contact:	
Full Name:		Contact:	
Form Completed by:		Signed:	
Approved by:		Signed:	

ACCIDENT / INCIDENT REPORT FORM

Incident Date:		Reported by:		Report Date:	
Incident Time:		Location:			

Person Involved /Injured:	Employee	Contractor	Visitor	General Public	Member	Other
Full Name:						
Address:						
Tel:			Email:			

DESCRIPTION OF ACCIDENT / INCIDENT

ACTION TAKEN / ACTIONS WHICH MAY PREVENT FUTURE REOCCURRENCE

WITNESS/ES

Full Name:		Contact:	
Full Name:		Contact:	
Full Name:		Contact:	
Form Completed by:		Signed:	
Approved by:		Signed:	

ACCIDENT / INCIDENT REPORT FORM

Incident Date:		Reported by:			Report Date:	
Incident Time:		Location:				

Person Involved /Injured:	Employee	Contractor	Visitor	General Public	Member	Other
Full Name:						
Address:						
Tel:			Email:			

DESCRIPTION OF ACCIDENT / INCIDENT

ACTION TAKEN / ACTIONS WHICH MAY PREVENT FUTURE REOCCURRENCE

WITNESS/ES

Full Name:		Contact:	
Full Name:		Contact:	
Full Name:		Contact:	
Form Completed by:		Signed:	
Approved by:		Signed:	

ACCIDENT / INCIDENT REPORT FORM

Incident Date:		Reported by:			Report Date:	
Incident Time:		Location:				

Person Involved /Injured:	Employee	Contractor	Visitor	General Public	Member	Other
Full Name:						
Address:						
Tel:			Email:			

DESCRIPTION OF ACCIDENT / INCIDENT

ACTION TAKEN / ACTIONS WHICH MAY PREVENT FUTURE REOCCURRENCE

WITNESS/ES

Full Name:		Contact:	
Full Name:		Contact:	
Full Name:		Contact:	
Form Completed by:		Signed:	
Approved by:		Signed:	

ACCIDENT / INCIDENT REPORT FORM

Incident Date:		Reported by:			Report Date:	
Incident Time:		Location:				

Person Involved /Injured:	Employee	Contractor	Visitor	General Public	Member	Other
Full Name:						
Address:						
Tel:			Email:			

DESCRIPTION OF ACCIDENT / INCIDENT

ACTION TAKEN / ACTIONS WHICH MAY PREVENT FUTURE REOCCURRENCE

WITNESS/ES

Full Name:		Contact:	
Full Name:		Contact:	
Full Name:		Contact:	
Form Completed by:		Signed:	
Approved by:		Signed:	

ACCIDENT / INCIDENT REPORT FORM

| Incident Date: | | Reported by: | | | Report Date: | |

| Incident Time: | | Location: | | | | |

Person Involved /Injured:	Employee	Contractor	Visitor	General Public	Member	Other
Full Name:						
Address:						
Tel:			Email:			

DESCRIPTION OF ACCIDENT / INCIDENT

ACTION TAKEN / ACTIONS WHICH MAY PREVENT FUTURE REOCCURRENCE

WITNESS/ES

Full Name:		Contact:	
Full Name:		Contact:	
Full Name:		Contact:	
Form Completed by:		Signed:	
Approved by:		Signed:	

ACCIDENT / INCIDENT REPORT FORM

| Incident Date: | | Reported by: | | | Report Date: | |
| Incident Time: | | Location: | | | | |

Person Involved /Injured:	Employee	Contractor	Visitor	General Public	Member	Other
Full Name:						
Address:						
Tel:			Email:			

DESCRIPTION OF ACCIDENT / INCIDENT

ACTION TAKEN / ACTIONS WHICH MAY PREVENT FUTURE REOCCURRENCE

WITNESS/ES

Full Name:		Contact:	
Full Name:		Contact:	
Full Name:		Contact:	
Form Completed by:		Signed:	
Approved by:		Signed:	

ACCIDENT / INCIDENT REPORT FORM

Incident Date:		Reported by:			Report Date:	
Incident Time:		Location:				

Person Involved /Injured:	Employee	Contractor	Visitor	General Public	Member	Other
Full Name:						
Address:						
Tel:			Email:			

DESCRIPTION OF ACCIDENT / INCIDENT

ACTION TAKEN / ACTIONS WHICH MAY PREVENT FUTURE REOCCURRENCE

WITNESS/ES

Full Name:		Contact:	
Full Name:		Contact:	
Full Name:		Contact:	
Form Completed by:		Signed:	
Approved by:		Signed:	

ACCIDENT / INCIDENT REPORT FORM

Incident Date:		Reported by:			Report Date:	
Incident Time:		Location:				

Person Involved /Injured:	Employee	Contractor	Visitor	General Public	Member	Other
Full Name:						
Address:						
Tel:			Email:			

DESCRIPTION OF ACCIDENT / INCIDENT

ACTION TAKEN / ACTIONS WHICH MAY PREVENT FUTURE REOCCURRENCE

WITNESS/ES

Full Name:		Contact:	
Full Name:		Contact:	
Full Name:		Contact:	
Form Completed by:		Signed:	
Approved by:		Signed:	

ACCIDENT / INCIDENT REPORT FORM

Incident Date:		Reported by:			Report Date:	
Incident Time:		Location:				

Person Involved /Injured:	Employee	Contractor	Visitor	General Public	Member	Other
Full Name:						
Address:						
Tel:			Email:			

DESCRIPTION OF ACCIDENT / INCIDENT

ACTION TAKEN / ACTIONS WHICH MAY PREVENT FUTURE REOCCURRENCE

WITNESS/ES

Full Name:		Contact:	
Full Name:		Contact:	
Full Name:		Contact:	
Form Completed by:		Signed:	
Approved by:		Signed:	

ACCIDENT / INCIDENT REPORT FORM

Incident Date:		Reported by:		Report Date:	
Incident Time:		Location:			

Person Involved /Injured:	Employee	Contractor	Visitor	General Public	Member	Other
Full Name:						
Address:						
Tel:			Email:			

DESCRIPTION OF ACCIDENT / INCIDENT

ACTION TAKEN / ACTIONS WHICH MAY PREVENT FUTURE REOCCURRENCE

WITNESS/ES

Full Name:		Contact:	
Full Name:		Contact:	
Full Name:		Contact:	
Form Completed by:		Signed:	
Approved by:		Signed:	

ACCIDENT / INCIDENT REPORT FORM

Incident Date:		Reported by:			Report Date:	

Incident Time:		Location:				

Person Involved /Injured:	Employee	Contractor	Visitor	General Public	Member	Other
Full Name:						
Address:						
Tel:			Email:			

DESCRIPTION OF ACCIDENT / INCIDENT

ACTION TAKEN / ACTIONS WHICH MAY PREVENT FUTURE REOCCURRENCE

WITNESS/ES

Full Name:		Contact:	
Full Name:		Contact:	
Full Name:		Contact:	
Form Completed by:		Signed:	
Approved by:		Signed:	

ACCIDENT / INCIDENT REPORT FORM

Incident Date:		Reported by:		Report Date:	
Incident Time:		Location:			

Person Involved /Injured:	Employee	Contractor	Visitor	General Public	Member	Other
Full Name:						
Address:						
Tel:		Email:				

DESCRIPTION OF ACCIDENT / INCIDENT

ACTION TAKEN / ACTIONS WHICH MAY PREVENT FUTURE REOCCURRENCE

WITNESS/ES

Full Name:		Contact:	
Full Name:		Contact:	
Full Name:		Contact:	
Form Completed by:		Signed:	
Approved by:		Signed:	

ACCIDENT / INCIDENT REPORT FORM

Incident Date:		Reported by:			Report Date:	
Incident Time:		Location:				

Person Involved /Injured:	Employee	Contractor	Visitor	General Public	Member	Other
Full Name:						
Address:						
Tel:			Email:			

DESCRIPTION OF ACCIDENT / INCIDENT

ACTION TAKEN / ACTIONS WHICH MAY PREVENT FUTURE REOCCURRENCE

WITNESS/ES

Full Name:		Contact:	
Full Name:		Contact:	
Full Name:		Contact:	
Form Completed by:		Signed:	
Approved by:		Signed:	

ACCIDENT / INCIDENT REPORT FORM

Incident Date:		Reported by:		Report Date:	

Incident Time:		Location:			

Person Involved /Injured:	Employee	Contractor	Visitor	General Public	Member	Other
Full Name:						
Address:						
Tel:		Email:				

DESCRIPTION OF ACCIDENT / INCIDENT

ACTION TAKEN / ACTIONS WHICH MAY PREVENT FUTURE REOCCURRENCE

WITNESS/ES

Full Name:		Contact:	
Full Name:		Contact:	
Full Name:		Contact:	
Form Completed by:		Signed:	
Approved by:		Signed:	

ACCIDENT / INCIDENT REPORT FORM

Incident Date:		Reported by:			Report Date:	
Incident Time:		Location:				

Person Involved /Injured:	Employee	Contractor	Visitor	General Public	Member	Other
Full Name:						
Address:						
Tel:			Email:			

DESCRIPTION OF ACCIDENT / INCIDENT

ACTION TAKEN / ACTIONS WHICH MAY PREVENT FUTURE REOCCURRENCE

WITNESS/ES

Full Name:		Contact:	
Full Name:		Contact:	
Full Name:		Contact:	
Form Completed by:		Signed:	
Approved by:		Signed:	

ACCIDENT / INCIDENT REPORT FORM

Incident Date:		Reported by:		Report Date:	
Incident Time:		Location:			

Person Involved /Injured:	Employee	Contractor	Visitor	General Public	Member	Other
Full Name:						
Address:						
Tel:		Email:				

DESCRIPTION OF ACCIDENT / INCIDENT

ACTION TAKEN / ACTIONS WHICH MAY PREVENT FUTURE REOCCURRENCE

WITNESS/ES

Full Name:		Contact:	
Full Name:		Contact:	
Full Name:		Contact:	
Form Completed by:		Signed:	
Approved by:		Signed:	

ACCIDENT / INCIDENT REPORT FORM

Incident Date:		Reported by:			Report Date:	
Incident Time:		Location:				

Person Involved /Injured:	Employee	Contractor	Visitor	General Public	Member	Other
Full Name:						
Address:						
Tel:			Email:			

DESCRIPTION OF ACCIDENT / INCIDENT

ACTION TAKEN / ACTIONS WHICH MAY PREVENT FUTURE REOCCURRENCE

WITNESS/ES

Full Name:		Contact:	
Full Name:		Contact:	
Full Name:		Contact:	
Form Completed by:		Signed:	
Approved by:		Signed:	

ACCIDENT / INCIDENT REPORT FORM

Incident Date:		Reported by:			Report Date:	
Incident Time:		Location:				

Person Involved /Injured:	Employee	Contractor	Visitor	General Public	Member	Other
Full Name:						
Address:						
Tel:			Email:			

DESCRIPTION OF ACCIDENT / INCIDENT

ACTION TAKEN / ACTIONS WHICH MAY PREVENT FUTURE REOCCURRENCE

WITNESS/ES

Full Name:		Contact:	
Full Name:		Contact:	
Full Name:		Contact:	
Form Completed by:		Signed:	
Approved by:		Signed:	

ACCIDENT / INCIDENT REPORT FORM

Incident Date:		Reported by:			Report Date:	

Incident Time:		Location:				

Person Involved /Injured:	Employee	Contractor	Visitor	General Public	Member	Other
Full Name:						
Address:						
Tel:		Email:				

DESCRIPTION OF ACCIDENT / INCIDENT

ACTION TAKEN / ACTIONS WHICH MAY PREVENT FUTURE REOCCURRENCE

WITNESS/ES

Full Name:		Contact:	
Full Name:		Contact:	
Full Name:		Contact:	
Form Completed by:		Signed:	
Approved by:		Signed:	

ACCIDENT / INCIDENT REPORT FORM

Incident Date:		Reported by:			Report Date:	
Incident Time:		Location:				

Person Involved /Injured:	Employee	Contractor	Visitor	General Public	Member	Other
Full Name:						
Address:						
Tel:			Email:			

DESCRIPTION OF ACCIDENT / INCIDENT

ACTION TAKEN / ACTIONS WHICH MAY PREVENT FUTURE REOCCURRENCE

WITNESS/ES

Full Name:		Contact:	
Full Name:		Contact:	
Full Name:		Contact:	
Form Completed by:		Signed:	
Approved by:		Signed:	

ACCIDENT / INCIDENT REPORT FORM

Incident Date:		Reported by:			Report Date:	
Incident Time:		Location:				

Person Involved /Injured:	Employee	Contractor	Visitor	General Public	Member	Other
Full Name:						
Address:						
Tel:			Email:			

DESCRIPTION OF ACCIDENT / INCIDENT

ACTION TAKEN / ACTIONS WHICH MAY PREVENT FUTURE REOCCURRENCE

WITNESS/ES

Full Name:		Contact:	
Full Name:		Contact:	
Full Name:		Contact:	
Form Completed by:		Signed:	
Approved by:		Signed:	

ACCIDENT / INCIDENT REPORT FORM

Incident Date:		Reported by:		Report Date:	
Incident Time:		Location:			

Person Involved /Injured:	Employee	Contractor	Visitor	General Public	Member	Other
Full Name:						
Address:						
Tel:			Email:			

DESCRIPTION OF ACCIDENT / INCIDENT

ACTION TAKEN / ACTIONS WHICH MAY PREVENT FUTURE REOCCURRENCE

WITNESS/ES

Full Name:		Contact:	
Full Name:		Contact:	
Full Name:		Contact:	
Form Completed by:		Signed:	
Approved by:		Signed:	

ACCIDENT / INCIDENT REPORT FORM

Incident Date:		Reported by:			Report Date:	
Incident Time:		Location:				

Person Involved /Injured:	Employee	Contractor	Visitor	General Public	Member	Other
Full Name:						
Address:						
Tel:		Email:				

DESCRIPTION OF ACCIDENT / INCIDENT

ACTION TAKEN / ACTIONS WHICH MAY PREVENT FUTURE REOCCURRENCE

WITNESS/ES

Full Name:		Contact:	
Full Name:		Contact:	
Full Name:		Contact:	
Form Completed by:		Signed:	
Approved by:		Signed:	

ACCIDENT / INCIDENT REPORT FORM

Incident Date:		Reported by:			Report Date:	
Incident Time:		Location:				

Person Involved /Injured:	Employee	Contractor	Visitor	General Public	Member	Other
Full Name:						
Address:						
Tel:			Email:			

DESCRIPTION OF ACCIDENT / INCIDENT

ACTION TAKEN / ACTIONS WHICH MAY PREVENT FUTURE REOCCURRENCE

WITNESS/ES

Full Name:		Contact:	
Full Name:		Contact:	
Full Name:		Contact:	
Form Completed by:		Signed:	
Approved by:		Signed:	

ACCIDENT / INCIDENT REPORT FORM

| Incident Date: | | Reported by: | | | Report Date: | |

| Incident Time: | | Location: | | | | |

Person Involved /Injured:	Employee	Contractor	Visitor	General Public	Member	Other
Full Name:						
Address:						
Tel:			Email:			

DESCRIPTION OF ACCIDENT / INCIDENT

ACTION TAKEN / ACTIONS WHICH MAY PREVENT FUTURE REOCCURRENCE

WITNESS/ES

Full Name:		Contact:	
Full Name:		Contact:	
Full Name:		Contact:	
Form Completed by:		Signed:	
Approved by:		Signed:	

ACCIDENT / INCIDENT REPORT FORM

Incident Date:		Reported by:		Report Date:	
Incident Time:		Location:			

Person Involved /Injured:	Employee	Contractor	Visitor	General Public	Member	Other
Full Name:						
Address:						
Tel:			Email:			

DESCRIPTION OF ACCIDENT / INCIDENT

ACTION TAKEN / ACTIONS WHICH MAY PREVENT FUTURE REOCCURRENCE

WITNESS/ES

Full Name:		Contact:	
Full Name:		Contact:	
Full Name:		Contact:	
Form Completed by:		Signed:	
Approved by:		Signed:	

ACCIDENT / INCIDENT REPORT FORM

Incident Date:		Reported by:			Report Date:	
Incident Time:		Location:				

Person Involved /Injured:	Employee	Contractor	Visitor	General Public	Member	Other
Full Name:						
Address:						
Tel:			Email:			

DESCRIPTION OF ACCIDENT / INCIDENT

ACTION TAKEN / ACTIONS WHICH MAY PREVENT FUTURE REOCCURRENCE

WITNESS/ES

Full Name:		Contact:	
Full Name:		Contact:	
Full Name:		Contact:	
Form Completed by:		Signed:	
Approved by:		Signed:	

ACCIDENT / INCIDENT REPORT FORM

Incident Date:		Reported by:			Report Date:	
Incident Time:		Location:				

Person Involved /Injured:	Employee	Contractor	Visitor	General Public	Member	Other
Full Name:						
Address:						
Tel:		Email:				

DESCRIPTION OF ACCIDENT / INCIDENT

ACTION TAKEN / ACTIONS WHICH MAY PREVENT FUTURE REOCCURRENCE

WITNESS/ES

Full Name:		Contact:	
Full Name:		Contact:	
Full Name:		Contact:	
Form Completed by:		Signed:	
Approved by:		Signed:	

ACCIDENT / INCIDENT REPORT FORM

Incident Date:		Reported by:			Report Date:	
Incident Time:		Location:				

Person Involved /Injured:	Employee	Contractor	Visitor	General Public	Member	Other
Full Name:						
Address:						
Tel:			Email:			

DESCRIPTION OF ACCIDENT / INCIDENT

ACTION TAKEN / ACTIONS WHICH MAY PREVENT FUTURE REOCCURRENCE

WITNESS/ES

Full Name:		Contact:	
Full Name:		Contact:	
Full Name:		Contact:	
Form Completed by:		Signed:	
Approved by:		Signed:	

ACCIDENT / INCIDENT REPORT FORM

Incident Date:		Reported by:		Report Date:	
Incident Time:		Location:			

Person Involved /Injured:	Employee	Contractor	Visitor	General Public	Member	Other
Full Name:						
Address:						
Tel:			Email:			

DESCRIPTION OF ACCIDENT / INCIDENT

ACTION TAKEN / ACTIONS WHICH MAY PREVENT FUTURE REOCCURRENCE

WITNESS/ES

Full Name:		Contact:	
Full Name:		Contact:	
Full Name:		Contact:	
Form Completed by:		Signed:	
Approved by:		Signed:	

ACCIDENT / INCIDENT REPORT FORM

Incident Date:		Reported by:			Report Date:	

Incident Time:		Location:				

Person Involved /Injured:	Employee	Contractor	Visitor	General Public	Member	Other
Full Name:						
Address:						
Tel:		Email:				

DESCRIPTION OF ACCIDENT / INCIDENT

ACTION TAKEN / ACTIONS WHICH MAY PREVENT FUTURE REOCCURRENCE

WITNESS/ES

Full Name:		Contact:	
Full Name:		Contact:	
Full Name:		Contact:	
Form Completed by:		Signed:	
Approved by:		Signed:	

ACCIDENT / INCIDENT REPORT FORM

Incident Date:		Reported by:		Report Date:	
Incident Time:		Location:			

Person Involved /Injured:	Employee	Contractor	Visitor	General Public	Member	Other
Full Name:						
Address:						
Tel:		Email:				

DESCRIPTION OF ACCIDENT / INCIDENT

ACTION TAKEN / ACTIONS WHICH MAY PREVENT FUTURE REOCCURRENCE

WITNESS/ES

Full Name:		Contact:	
Full Name:		Contact:	
Full Name:		Contact:	
Form Completed by:		Signed:	
Approved by:		Signed:	

ACCIDENT / INCIDENT REPORT FORM

Incident Date:		Reported by:			Report Date:	
Incident Time:		Location:				

Person Involved /Injured:	Employee	Contractor	Visitor	General Public	Member	Other
Full Name:						
Address:						
Tel:			Email:			

DESCRIPTION OF ACCIDENT / INCIDENT

ACTION TAKEN / ACTIONS WHICH MAY PREVENT FUTURE REOCCURRENCE

WITNESS/ES

Full Name:		Contact:	
Full Name:		Contact:	
Full Name:		Contact:	
Form Completed by:		Signed:	
Approved by:		Signed:	

ACCIDENT / INCIDENT REPORT FORM

Incident Date:		Reported by:			Report Date:	

Incident Time:		Location:				

Person Involved /Injured:	Employee	Contractor	Visitor	General Public	Member	Other
Full Name:						
Address:						
Tel:			Email:			

DESCRIPTION OF ACCIDENT / INCIDENT

ACTION TAKEN / ACTIONS WHICH MAY PREVENT FUTURE REOCCURRENCE

WITNESS/ES

Full Name:		Contact:	
Full Name:		Contact:	
Full Name:		Contact:	
Form Completed by:		Signed:	
Approved by:		Signed:	

ACCIDENT / INCIDENT REPORT FORM

Incident Date:		Reported by:			Report Date:	
Incident Time:		Location:				

Person Involved /Injured:	Employee	Contractor	Visitor	General Public	Member	Other
Full Name:						
Address:						
Tel:			Email:			

DESCRIPTION OF ACCIDENT / INCIDENT

ACTION TAKEN / ACTIONS WHICH MAY PREVENT FUTURE REOCCURRENCE

WITNESS/ES

Full Name:		Contact:	
Full Name:		Contact:	
Full Name:		Contact:	
Form Completed by:		Signed:	
Approved by:		Signed:	

ACCIDENT / INCIDENT REPORT FORM

Incident Date:		Reported by:			Report Date:	

Incident Time:		Location:				

Person Involved /Injured:	Employee	Contractor	Visitor	General Public	Member	Other
Full Name:						
Address:						
Tel:			Email:			

DESCRIPTION OF ACCIDENT / INCIDENT

ACTION TAKEN / ACTIONS WHICH MAY PREVENT FUTURE REOCCURRENCE

WITNESS/ES

Full Name:		Contact:	
Full Name:		Contact:	
Full Name:		Contact:	
Form Completed by:		Signed:	
Approved by:		Signed:	

ACCIDENT / INCIDENT REPORT FORM

Incident Date:		Reported by:			Report Date:	
Incident Time:		Location:				

Person Involved /Injured:	Employee	Contractor	Visitor	General Public	Member	Other
Full Name:						
Address:						
Tel:			Email:			

DESCRIPTION OF ACCIDENT / INCIDENT

ACTION TAKEN / ACTIONS WHICH MAY PREVENT FUTURE REOCCURRENCE

WITNESS/ES

Full Name:		Contact:	
Full Name:		Contact:	
Full Name:		Contact:	
Form Completed by:		Signed:	
Approved by:		Signed:	

ACCIDENT / INCIDENT REPORT FORM

Incident Date:		Reported by:			Report Date:	
Incident Time:		Location:				

Person Involved /Injured:	Employee	Contractor	Visitor	General Public	Member	Other
Full Name:						
Address:						
Tel:			Email:			

DESCRIPTION OF ACCIDENT / INCIDENT

ACTION TAKEN / ACTIONS WHICH MAY PREVENT FUTURE REOCCURRENCE

WITNESS/ES

Full Name:		Contact:	
Full Name:		Contact:	
Full Name:		Contact:	
Form Completed by:		Signed:	
Approved by:		Signed:	

ACCIDENT / INCIDENT REPORT FORM

Incident Date:		Reported by:			Report Date:	
Incident Time:		Location:				

Person Involved /Injured:	Employee	Contractor	Visitor	General Public	Member	Other
Full Name:						
Address:						
Tel:			Email:			

DESCRIPTION OF ACCIDENT / INCIDENT

ACTION TAKEN / ACTIONS WHICH MAY PREVENT FUTURE REOCCURRENCE

WITNESS/ES

Full Name:		Contact:	
Full Name:		Contact:	
Full Name:		Contact:	
Form Completed by:		Signed:	
Approved by:		Signed:	

ACCIDENT / INCIDENT REPORT FORM

Incident Date:		Reported by:			Report Date:	
Incident Time:		Location:				

Person Involved /Injured:	Employee	Contractor	Visitor	General Public	Member	Other
Full Name:						
Address:						
Tel:			Email:			

DESCRIPTION OF ACCIDENT / INCIDENT

ACTION TAKEN / ACTIONS WHICH MAY PREVENT FUTURE REOCCURRENCE

WITNESS/ES

Full Name:		Contact:	
Full Name:		Contact:	
Full Name:		Contact:	
Form Completed by:		Signed:	
Approved by:		Signed:	

ACCIDENT / INCIDENT REPORT FORM

Incident Date:		Reported by:			Report Date:	
Incident Time:		Location:				

Person Involved /Injured:	Employee	Contractor	Visitor	General Public	Member	Other
Full Name:						
Address:						
Tel:			Email:			

DESCRIPTION OF ACCIDENT / INCIDENT

ACTION TAKEN / ACTIONS WHICH MAY PREVENT FUTURE REOCCURRENCE

WITNESS/ES

Full Name:		Contact:	
Full Name:		Contact:	
Full Name:		Contact:	
Form Completed by:		Signed:	
Approved by:		Signed:	

ACCIDENT / INCIDENT REPORT FORM

Incident Date:		Reported by:			Report Date:	
Incident Time:		Location:				

Person Involved /Injured:	Employee	Contractor	Visitor	General Public	Member	Other
Full Name:						
Address:						
Tel:			Email:			

DESCRIPTION OF ACCIDENT / INCIDENT

ACTION TAKEN / ACTIONS WHICH MAY PREVENT FUTURE REOCCURRENCE

WITNESS/ES

Full Name:		Contact:	
Full Name:		Contact:	
Full Name:		Contact:	
Form Completed by:		Signed:	
Approved by:		Signed:	

ACCIDENT / INCIDENT REPORT FORM

Incident Date:		Reported by:			Report Date:	
Incident Time:		Location:				

Person Involved /Injured:	Employee	Contractor	Visitor	General Public	Member	Other
Full Name:						
Address:						
Tel:			Email:			

DESCRIPTION OF ACCIDENT / INCIDENT

ACTION TAKEN / ACTIONS WHICH MAY PREVENT FUTURE REOCCURRENCE

WITNESS/ES

Full Name:		Contact:	
Full Name:		Contact:	
Full Name:		Contact:	
Form Completed by:		Signed:	
Approved by:		Signed:	

ACCIDENT / INCIDENT REPORT FORM

| Incident Date: | | Reported by: | | | Report Date: | |

| Incident Time: | | Location: | | | | |

Person Involved /Injured:	Employee	Contractor	Visitor	General Public	Member	Other
Full Name:						
Address:						
Tel:			Email:			

DESCRIPTION OF ACCIDENT / INCIDENT

ACTION TAKEN / ACTIONS WHICH MAY PREVENT FUTURE REOCCURRENCE

WITNESS/ES

Full Name:		Contact:	
Full Name:		Contact:	
Full Name:		Contact:	
Form Completed by:		Signed:	
Approved by:		Signed:	

ACCIDENT / INCIDENT REPORT FORM

Incident Date:		Reported by:			Report Date:	
Incident Time:		Location:				

Person Involved /Injured:	Employee	Contractor	Visitor	General Public	Member	Other
Full Name:						
Address:						
Tel:		Email:				

DESCRIPTION OF ACCIDENT / INCIDENT

ACTION TAKEN / ACTIONS WHICH MAY PREVENT FUTURE REOCCURRENCE

WITNESS/ES

Full Name:		Contact:	
Full Name:		Contact:	
Full Name:		Contact:	
Form Completed by:		Signed:	
Approved by:		Signed:	

ACCIDENT / INCIDENT REPORT FORM

Incident Date:		Reported by:		Report Date:	
Incident Time:		Location:			

Person Involved /Injured:	Employee	Contractor	Visitor	General Public	Member	Other
Full Name:						
Address:						
Tel:			Email:			

DESCRIPTION OF ACCIDENT / INCIDENT

ACTION TAKEN / ACTIONS WHICH MAY PREVENT FUTURE REOCCURRENCE

WITNESS/ES

Full Name:		Contact:	
Full Name:		Contact:	
Full Name:		Contact:	
Form Completed by:		Signed:	
Approved by:		Signed:	

ACCIDENT / INCIDENT REPORT FORM

Incident Date:		Reported by:			Report Date:	
Incident Time:		Location:				

Person Involved /Injured:	Employee	Contractor	Visitor	General Public	Member	Other
Full Name:						
Address:						
Tel:			Email:			

DESCRIPTION OF ACCIDENT / INCIDENT

ACTION TAKEN / ACTIONS WHICH MAY PREVENT FUTURE REOCCURRENCE

WITNESS/ES

Full Name:		Contact:	
Full Name:		Contact:	
Full Name:		Contact:	
Form Completed by:		Signed:	
Approved by:		Signed:	

ACCIDENT / INCIDENT REPORT FORM

Incident Date:		Reported by:			Report Date:	
Incident Time:		Location:				

Person Involved /Injured:	Employee	Contractor	Visitor	General Public	Member	Other
Full Name:						
Address:						
Tel:		Email:				

DESCRIPTION OF ACCIDENT / INCIDENT

ACTION TAKEN / ACTIONS WHICH MAY PREVENT FUTURE REOCCURRENCE

WITNESS/ES

Full Name:		Contact:	
Full Name:		Contact:	
Full Name:		Contact:	
Form Completed by:		Signed:	
Approved by:		Signed:	

ACCIDENT / INCIDENT REPORT FORM

Incident Date:		Reported by:			Report Date:	
Incident Time:		Location:				

Person Involved /Injured:	Employee	Contractor	Visitor	General Public	Member	Other
Full Name:						
Address:						
Tel:			Email:			

DESCRIPTION OF ACCIDENT / INCIDENT

ACTION TAKEN / ACTIONS WHICH MAY PREVENT FUTURE REOCCURRENCE

WITNESS/ES

Full Name:		Contact:	
Full Name:		Contact:	
Full Name:		Contact:	
Form Completed by:		Signed:	
Approved by:		Signed:	

ACCIDENT / INCIDENT REPORT FORM

Incident Date:		Reported by:			Report Date:	
Incident Time:		Location:				

Person Involved /Injured:	Employee	Contractor	Visitor	General Public	Member	Other
Full Name:						
Address:						
Tel:			Email:			

DESCRIPTION OF ACCIDENT / INCIDENT

ACTION TAKEN / ACTIONS WHICH MAY PREVENT FUTURE REOCCURRENCE

WITNESS/ES

Full Name:		Contact:	
Full Name:		Contact:	
Full Name:		Contact:	
Form Completed by:		Signed:	
Approved by:		Signed:	

ACCIDENT / INCIDENT REPORT FORM

Incident Date:		Reported by:			Report Date:	
Incident Time:		Location:				

Person Involved /Injured:	Employee	Contractor	Visitor	General Public	Member	Other
Full Name:						
Address:						
Tel:			Email:			

DESCRIPTION OF ACCIDENT / INCIDENT

ACTION TAKEN / ACTIONS WHICH MAY PREVENT FUTURE REOCCURRENCE

WITNESS/ES

Full Name:		Contact:	
Full Name:		Contact:	
Full Name:		Contact:	
Form Completed by:		Signed:	
Approved by:		Signed:	

ACCIDENT / INCIDENT REPORT FORM

Incident Date:		Reported by:			Report Date:	
Incident Time:		Location:				

Person Involved /Injured:	Employee	Contractor	Visitor	General Public	Member	Other
Full Name:						
Address:						
Tel:			Email:			

DESCRIPTION OF ACCIDENT / INCIDENT

ACTION TAKEN / ACTIONS WHICH MAY PREVENT FUTURE REOCCURRENCE

WITNESS/ES

Full Name:		Contact:	
Full Name:		Contact:	
Full Name:		Contact:	
Form Completed by:		Signed:	
Approved by:		Signed:	

ACCIDENT / INCIDENT REPORT FORM

Incident Date:		Reported by:			Report Date:	
Incident Time:		Location:				

Person Involved /Injured:	Employee	Contractor	Visitor	General Public	Member	Other
Full Name:						
Address:						
Tel:			Email:			

DESCRIPTION OF ACCIDENT / INCIDENT

ACTION TAKEN / ACTIONS WHICH MAY PREVENT FUTURE REOCCURRENCE

WITNESS/ES

Full Name:		Contact:	
Full Name:		Contact:	
Full Name:		Contact:	
Form Completed by:		Signed:	
Approved by:		Signed:	

ACCIDENT / INCIDENT REPORT FORM

Incident Date:		Reported by:			Report Date:	
Incident Time:		Location:				

Person Involved /Injured:	Employee	Contractor	Visitor	General Public	Member	Other
Full Name:						
Address:						
Tel:			Email:			

DESCRIPTION OF ACCIDENT / INCIDENT

ACTION TAKEN / ACTIONS WHICH MAY PREVENT FUTURE REOCCURRENCE

WITNESS/ES

Full Name:		Contact:	
Full Name:		Contact:	
Full Name:		Contact:	
Form Completed by:		Signed:	
Approved by:		Signed:	

ACCIDENT / INCIDENT REPORT FORM

Incident Date:		Reported by:			Report Date:	
Incident Time:		Location:				

Person Involved /Injured:	Employee	Contractor	Visitor	General Public	Member	Other
Full Name:						
Address:						
Tel:		Email:				

DESCRIPTION OF ACCIDENT / INCIDENT

ACTION TAKEN / ACTIONS WHICH MAY PREVENT FUTURE REOCCURRENCE

WITNESS/ES

Full Name:		Contact:	
Full Name:		Contact:	
Full Name:		Contact:	
Form Completed by:		Signed:	
Approved by:		Signed:	

ACCIDENT / INCIDENT REPORT FORM

Incident Date:		Reported by:		Report Date:	
Incident Time:		Location:			

Person Involved /Injured:	Employee	Contractor	Visitor	General Public	Member	Other
Full Name:						
Address:						
Tel:			Email:			

DESCRIPTION OF ACCIDENT / INCIDENT

ACTION TAKEN / ACTIONS WHICH MAY PREVENT FUTURE REOCCURRENCE

WITNESS/ES

Full Name:		Contact:	
Full Name:		Contact:	
Full Name:		Contact:	
Form Completed by:		Signed:	
Approved by:		Signed:	

ACCIDENT / INCIDENT REPORT FORM

| Incident Date: | | Reported by: | | | Report Date: | |
| Incident Time: | | Location: | | | | |

Person Involved /Injured:	Employee	Contractor	Visitor	General Public	Member	Other
Full Name:						
Address:						
Tel:			Email:			

DESCRIPTION OF ACCIDENT / INCIDENT

ACTION TAKEN / ACTIONS WHICH MAY PREVENT FUTURE REOCCURRENCE

WITNESS/ES

Full Name:		Contact:	
Full Name:		Contact:	
Full Name:		Contact:	
Form Completed by:		Signed:	
Approved by:		Signed:	

ACCIDENT / INCIDENT REPORT FORM

| Incident Date: | | Reported by: | | | Report Date: | |

| Incident Time: | | Location: | | | | |

Person Involved /Injured:	Employee	Contractor	Visitor	General Public	Member	Other
Full Name:						
Address:						
Tel:			Email:			

DESCRIPTION OF ACCIDENT / INCIDENT

ACTION TAKEN / ACTIONS WHICH MAY PREVENT FUTURE REOCCURRENCE

WITNESS/ES

Full Name:		Contact:	
Full Name:		Contact:	
Full Name:		Contact:	
Form Completed by:		Signed:	
Approved by:		Signed:	

ACCIDENT / INCIDENT REPORT FORM

Incident Date:		Reported by:			Report Date:	
Incident Time:		Location:				

Person Involved /Injured:	Employee	Contractor	Visitor	General Public	Member	Other
Full Name:						
Address:						
Tel:			Email:			

DESCRIPTION OF ACCIDENT / INCIDENT

ACTION TAKEN / ACTIONS WHICH MAY PREVENT FUTURE REOCCURRENCE

WITNESS/ES

Full Name:		Contact:	
Full Name:		Contact:	
Full Name:		Contact:	
Form Completed by:		Signed:	
Approved by:		Signed:	

ACCIDENT / INCIDENT REPORT FORM

| Incident Date: | | Reported by: | | | Report Date: | |

| Incident Time: | | Location: | | | | |

Person Involved /Injured:	Employee	Contractor	Visitor	General Public	Member	Other
Full Name:						
Address:						
Tel:			Email:			

DESCRIPTION OF ACCIDENT / INCIDENT

ACTION TAKEN / ACTIONS WHICH MAY PREVENT FUTURE REOCCURRENCE

WITNESS/ES

Full Name:		Contact:	
Full Name:		Contact:	
Full Name:		Contact:	
Form Completed by:		Signed:	
Approved by:		Signed:	

ACCIDENT / INCIDENT REPORT FORM

Incident Date:		Reported by:			Report Date:	
Incident Time:		Location:				

Person Involved /Injured:	Employee	Contractor	Visitor	General Public	Member	Other
Full Name:						
Address:						
Tel:			Email:			

DESCRIPTION OF ACCIDENT / INCIDENT

ACTION TAKEN / ACTIONS WHICH MAY PREVENT FUTURE REOCCURRENCE

WITNESS/ES

Full Name:		Contact:	
Full Name:		Contact:	
Full Name:		Contact:	
Form Completed by:		Signed:	
Approved by:		Signed:	

ACCIDENT / INCIDENT REPORT FORM

| Incident Date: | | Reported by: | | | Report Date: | |
| Incident Time: | | Location: | | | | |

Person Involved /Injured:	Employee	Contractor	Visitor	General Public	Member	Other
Full Name:						
Address:						
Tel:			Email:			

DESCRIPTION OF ACCIDENT / INCIDENT

ACTION TAKEN / ACTIONS WHICH MAY PREVENT FUTURE REOCCURRENCE

WITNESS/ES

Full Name:		Contact:	
Full Name:		Contact:	
Full Name:		Contact:	
Form Completed by:		Signed:	
Approved by:		Signed:	

Made in the USA
Las Vegas, NV
14 May 2024